RAINBOW DANCER

RAINBOW DANCER

HEATHER HARRIS

CAITLIN PRESS

Published by
Caitlin Press
Box 2387, Stn. B
Prince George, BC V2N 2S6

Caitlin Press acknowledges the financial support of the
Canada Council for the Arts for our publishing program.
Similarly, we acknowledge the support of the Arts Council
of British Columbia.

Cover design by Gaye Hammond
Page design and output by David Lee Communications
Cover photo by Bobbi Koll
Photo of Heather Harris with daughters Jessie and
Charlotte by W.D. West Studios

Canadian Cataloguing in Publication Data

Harris, Heather, 1953–
Rainbow Dancer

Poems
ISBN 0-920576-76-1

I. Title
PS8565.A64865R34 1999   C811'.54   C99-910611-2
PR9199.3.H3459R34 1999

THE CANADA COUNCIL | LE CONSEIL DES ARTS
FOR THE ARTS | DU CANADA
SINCE 1957 | DEPUIS 1957

CONTENTS

ACKNOWLEDGEMENTS

To my mother
Claire Irene Yule (Pattenaude)
1931-1999
who never got to hear my poems

THESE POEMS REPRESENT my forty-five years of experience and the experiences of 10,000 years of our ancestors. Many of the poems tell actual stories from my life and the lives of my friends and relatives. All of these stories are true just as all Raven stories are true. As I was once told by Gitxsan chief David Harris, Xhlex, "Andamatlasxw (Raven stories) are half way between a joke and a lie but they're all true anyway." So, too, are my stories.

I would like to thank everyone who gave me these gifts of memories which have made my life so rich. The list is long but includes: my mother, Claire Yule, who passed away recently; my father, Alex Yule, who passed away in 1996; my grandmother, Jessie Comer, who moved on in 1988; my children Alex, Charlotte (Four Winds Woman), and Jessie (Little Elk Woman); my husband and love, Leon Sadownik, who I dragged into a new reality; my ex-husband, David Harris, and all my Gitxsan in-laws (especially the late Mary Johnson, Antgwulilibiksxw, the most knowledgeable lady I ever knew); my friend and brother in arms, Ward Churchill, who continues to inspire me to do good things; Aaju Peter of Iqlauit (Aaju's Kitchen); Milton Freeman (Nylon Rope): Art Wilson, Wii Mugulsxw (Fish Wars); Oscar Dennis (Summer Songbook); Ray LeBlanc and Sheila Greer (The Dinner Party); Alfred Joseph, Gisdaywa (Alfred's Story); and Percy Sterritt, Wii Baaxw, for telling me the best story I ever heard. Oh, and Arnie, who like me, always has hope.

Special thanks to Charlie Schweger who sent me a book by Wendy Rose to which my reaction was, "I can do that" and I did.

Special thanks to Bobbie Koll, Arlene Mackinaw, Dave Arnold and the rest of the Rainbow Dancers.

I would also like to thank Barb Munk, Cynthia Wilson and Melanie Callahan of Caitlin Press for turning my stories into a book.

Lastly, I must thank the Creator, Coyote and Wii Gyet without whom I wouldn't be here.

And I send my prayers to all the people who fight on for justice.

—Heather Harris

A Dance for Future Generations

I want my words to be as eloquent
As the sound of a rattle snake.

I want my actions to be as direct
As the strike of a rattle snake.

I want the results as conclusive
As the bite of a beautiful red and black coral snake.

—Jimmie Durham
"Columbus Day"

POETRY IS UNDOUBTEDLY the literate world's closest approximation of the oral traditions by which indigenous societies have always defined themselves. This is perhaps why, amidst the "American Indian Renaissance" which is said to have occurred since the mid-1960s, poets have played a singularly substantial role, sometimes threatening by the sheer power embodied in their attainments to overshadow contributions offered through other media. The list of those fitting this description, while not especially long, evidences a clear and penetrating luminance, including as it does the likes of Simon J. Ortiz and Chrystos, Adrian C. Louis and Wendy Rose, Elizabeth Woody and Joy Harjo, Barney Bush and Carter Revard, Mary Tall Mountain and Peter Blue Cloud, Linda Hogan and Maurice Kenny.

Comes now Heather Harris and *Rainbow Dancer*, a collection of poems so strong, so compelling, so unequivocally vital as to capture—indeed, to incarnate—the very essence of an ancient and collective wisdom cast up in all its primal vibrancy upon the pocked terrain of socio-literary postmodernism. The verse is tough, honest, sinewy, uncompromising in its finality, yet simultaneously imbued with such gentleness, such tenderness of purpose as to transcend the intellectual/moral stultification with which contemporary existence has become so deeply afflicted, providing instead that most elusive of all prospects: hope.

The book is thus, as it should and must be, many things, many voices, each and all of them drawn into a harmony so irrefutable as to echo the sounds of the wind upon the buffalo grass.

Rainbow Dancer is first of all an honouring song—a testimony to and a prayer for ancestors whose struggles against the predatory madness of an invading culture have been carried from generation to generation over five centuries. There were struggles that were at the cost of incalculable suffering, not simply to repel or survive the relentlessly genocidal onslaught but to sustain the very possibility of natural equilibrium in the face of what the Hopis have come to call "Koyaanisqatsi."

So too is the poetry an embrace and salute, a fervent enunciation of respect and solidarity with those today who assert the inherent continuity of that which was and that which remains, apprehending and comporting themselves in the spirit of Crazy Horse and Tecumseh, Almighty Voice and Black Buffalo Woman. They are willing of necessity to pay the price of their resistance, establishing themselves in eternal remembrance as beacons shining undaunted and undiminished through a twilight that, without them, might harken the blank endlessness of a truly ecocidal night.

Most of all, in laying bare these linkages joining Native past to Native present, Harris reveals the bedrock upon which both are, or can be, connected to the Native future as well. Hers is thus, and most importantly, a celebratory verbal dance devoted to the welcoming of a new dawn birthing

10

among coming generations. Upon them as well as us she bestows, as Native women always have or with justice always will, the gifts of her vision, her courage, her dignity and the integrity of her unflinching dedication neither to forget nor to surrender that which is hers, and, by extension, theirs to inherit. No greater tribute can be asked or offered.

—Ward Churchill
July 1999

Dr. Ward Churchill is Creek-Cherokee (a member of Keetoowah Band Cherokee). He is one of the strongest and most influential voices of native resistance to colonial oppression in North America. He is both an activist and an intellectual defending the rights of indigenous people across North America and around the world. Dr. Churchill is the Coordinator of American Studies at the Center for Studies of Race and Ethnicity in America at the University of Colorado at Boulder; he is co-director of the Colorado chapter of the American Indian Movement and vice-chair of the American Anti-Defamation Council; he has served as a delegate to the United Nations Working Group on Indigenous Populations and has served with many other organizations protecting the interests of aboriginal people. Dr. Churchill is a prolific writer on issues affecting indigenous peoples. He has written innumerable articles and many books including Fantasies of the Master Race, Indians Are Us?, Struggle for the Land, *and* Since Predator Came.

1: Indian Humour

Indian Humour

White people see Native people

as stoic, humourless.

We think that's pretty funny.
What's funny to us isn't funny to them.

Novelty is humourous to white folks.
To Indians it's the familiar.
Nothing funnier than a reference
to an old joke.

A many times told joke.

Humour's been with us forever.

Even before that.

Old Man Coyote brought us humour.
He liked a good joke more than most.
Otherwise he wouldn't have changed
things the way he did.

The world's different since
Old Coyote walked the earth.

Our lives have been pretty rough.
Humour helps us to get by.

Did you hear about the time Coyote's brother Raven
saw three nice bears? Decided to make a coat out
of them. He tore up his old Raven coat but those
bears got away. Raven ended up with no coat at all.

Did you hear Basil Johnson tell about the Moose Meat
Point Indians lassoing a moose?

That's a good one.

Did you hear the one about the Indian guy
meeting a beautiful white woman?
She tells him Indians and Irishmen
are the best lovers.

He says, "Ma'am, meet Tonto O'Reilly."

Did you hear the one about Columbus
discovering America?
That's a real joke.

Nothing like a good laugh to keep you going.

POLAR MAN

I saw many wonders
in that northern town.

Caribou grazing in the front yard.
Forty below in April.
Frozen sea in July.

Polar Man.

Saw him first on a cold day.
Dressed for forty or fifty degrees warmer.
Suitable for what I'm not sure.

Picture him:

White sweatshirt, white sweatpants
with black shorts over top.
Black boots, gloves and mask.

Polar Man.

When I asked about him.
"His mind is not quite right.
He used to be Polar Boy.
Now he's Polar Man."

We met him one day.
My husband said,
"You look like Batman."

Polar Man replied,
"You look like a tourist."

An acuity not usually attributable
to those whose minds are not quite right.

Food Acculturated Little Indian

Frozen hairy moose nose
thawing in a pan
on the kitchen counter.

"Hey, Mom, what's that?"

"It's a moose nose."

"What's it for?"

"Daddy's going to eat it."

"————He is nooot!"

ARNIE TRIED TO PICK ME UP AT MY DAD'S FUNERAL

My pretty white boyfriend
drove me crazy
when I was twenty.

Party guy.
Full of jokes and empty flattery.
Golden-haired lover.
Drank too much,
borrowed money.
Loved women,
any women.

I moved far away.
Geographically, culturally, socially.

More than twenty years went by.
Married.
Had kids, degrees, jobs.

One day my dad passed away.
We went to bury him in his home town.
My childhood home.

Arnie showed up at the funeral
Same face, same haircut,
same Arnie.

Glued to me at the wake.
Cracking jokes.
"Hey!
Did you hear Lorena Bobbit
was killed in a car accident yesterday?
Some prick cut her off!"

I am a woman in love with my husband.
Three great kids, good job.
Arnie has no money, no job,
no home, no assets.
Been living off women
for the twenty years
since I last saw him.

Arnie's got hope.
Trying to pick me up

at my dad's funeral.

First Serious Snowfall of the Year

Is this
the northern part of south
or the southern part of north?

Fifty-four degrees more or less.

Relative.

South to Inuvik friends.
North of where U. S. ends.

I went to work coatless on Monday.
We had our first snowfall on Sunday.

I won't curse the snow.
Our elders told us stories
of what befalls those who do.

When I'm rich and famous
like Buffy St. Marie.
I think I'll move to
the sun-lit snow-free tropics

of Hawaii.

COYOTE, WHERE ARE YOU?

Where are you now, Coyote?
I've heard a lot about where you've been.
Learned a few things from you
Had a few laughs at your expense.
Where are you now?

They say you are still around.
I've never seen you.

Or maybe I have.

Was it you who sweet talked me,
Stole my wallet that time?

Who stole my car that day?

I thought I saw a guy in a fur hat
driving it away.

Was it you who introduced
a younger prettier girl
to the boyfriend I was crazy about?

I have seen you, Coyote.

FAMILIAR COYOTE

Never lived in Coyote's country
or heard Coyote stories on grandmother's knee.

Always lived in Raven's Country.
Heard about his wisdom and his folly.

Coyote sounds, looks, feels so familiar.
More familiar than his Raven relative
I've met so many times.

Even bore a child who has been
accused of being Raven.
He doesn't ring a psychic bell.
Coyote does.

Keep hearing him scratch at my windows
and my consciousness at night
Seeing the shadow of the tip of his tail
slip around the corner.
Smelling his faint musty fur.
Not finding the source.

Maybe Coyote came with the coyote hide
I bought to sew mitts and hats with.

Maybe that's why I couldn't cut it up.
Left it whole upon my shelf.

That hide watches me with empty eyes.
Managing to invite attention,
affection,
with his fluffy fur.
even after death.

I half expect that hide
to fill out, come to life.
Stand up, try to talk me out of my lunch.

Or into my skirt.

My Cree, Metis and Gitxsan relatives
haven't told me of Coyote.

I had an *Aatsina* grandmother long ago.

Maybe she sent Coyote to me
so I won't forget her.

II: What's Theirs is Theirs and What's Ours is Theirs

Appropriating Self

I saw a picture of a native guy.

He laid himself out
as a museum display in Santa Barbara.

He made himself an artifact

along with his pipe, his car keys,
his medicine bag, his credit card.

The people who came to the museum
to see artifacts
were amused, angry, uncomfortable.

Looking at themselves
looking at him.

They had often stared uncaring
at his relatives.

I dance for people.

Some are open of mind and heart
wanting to learn.

Others want only a trophy photograph.

"Seen the Indians,
bin there, dun that."

I wonder if I should do this?

Be an artifact
like the guy in Santa Barbara?

NYLON ROPE

A room full of people of many minds
listened to a knowledgeable man
speak of whales, Inuit and Inuit whaling.
How those people of the sea
take a living from that difficult land
still have time to love, laugh and create.

They love that hard land profoundly
and the creatures there
that provide them with food, clothing, shelter,
most other needs.
An astounding feat given the long months
of cold and dark,
the great distances to travel.

The love the people have for their prey
unites them in a sacred bond.
Each providing for the other.
Every hunter giving thanks
for the gift of flesh
the animals provide
when respect for them is proffered.

North the whiteman went in his avarice.
Slaughtering the whales for profit.
Giving no thanks for the great gift.

The people carried on struggling
to feed their families.

Following the southern whalers,
missionaries, government agents and teachers.
Camp people herded into new villages
more easily administered.

Expensive southern food imported.
Country food still essential to survival.
The people carried on hunting, eating whales
in that sacred cycle of life the man tells us.

After he speaks,
a woman who refused to hear,
a southern woman well fed on beef and pork,
wrapped in Styrofoam and cellophane
says for who care to listen:
"They are not Inuit anymore
because they have nylon rope."

She has proclaimed herself
the Grand Arbitrator of Cultural Authenticity.

Makes decisions on the purity of cultures.
Decides the cultural beliefs
and practices of people she has never met.
Decides on others' right to eat.

People brought up in climate-controlled surroundings.

Brought up on limitless store-bought food
agree with her.

The Native Women's Movement

Why aren't there any native women
in the women's' movement?

A short answer.

Native women are too busy living life
to talk about it.

Many struggle to survive.

The issue of sexist language
is real low on their priority list.

When your kids eat rice and fish
for weeks,
cry for juice and cereal.

When it's been thirty below
for a week,
you're out of fire wood.

When only a few dozen
out of a few hundred
in your village
have a job.

When your daughter starts
drinking at thirteen.

Your son is arrested
at fourteen.

It's hard to think
about feminist issues.

It's easy to think
about human issues.

To think about how those who
have time to think about
the issues
are members of the society
that put your society
in this position.

How not so many years ago
your people were healthy
and self-sufficient.
With a secure future to

look forward to.

How control of the land
on which your people made
their living
for thousands of years
was so suddenly and completely
taken away.

The wealth of your land
flows into the hands of others

They disparage you for
accepting a six hundred dollar
welfare cheque

to feed a family of six.

Easy to think about
how those of us
who are independent
work twice as hard

for half as much.

We don't have time to think
about the women's movement.

We only have time to get things done.

SQUATTERS ON THEIR OWN LAND

Hawai'ian Islands' breath-taking beauty
intoxicates me.

Oahu:

Thunderous surf on North Beach.
Crazed daredevils riding scraps
of fiberglass
on moving water mountains.

Glittering, shimmering bits
of flashing colour.

Not like the solid salmon
of our northern waters
around my feet at Hanauma Bay.

Kawaii:

Desert dryness at Poipou Beach.
Saturated tropical lushness at
Waimea Mountain.
Red rocked Grand Canyon at Waimea.
Cliffs drop from my feet
straight down to Napali Valley's floor.

Clouds drift far below me
in the valley where the *ali'i*
of Kawaii once resided.
The blue of water and sky
blur together horizonless.

Although twenty years have passed
I still feel euphoric from the memory
of the beauty of those islands.

A traveller from a colder place
with a very different kind of beauty.
Privileged to be given the gift
of a visit to such a place.

To be able to share this beauty is an honour.

Camping by the sea
among the ironwood trees at Wailua.

A family of this place
camp beside us.
Friendly and kind
they welcome us.
They share fish they have
caught in the sea
with small nets thrown by the men.

They feed us purple poi.
A food we have never seen before.

They laugh with us.
Sing for us.
Tell us they no longer
own their homeland.
Others have usurped them.
Have taken up the land
to build hotels, shops, attractions.

They have no American money
to buy back some of their land
where they can live
their own way in peace.

Their land is in great demand.
Property values are very high.
The Hawai'ians are squatters
on their own land.
Reduced to living
in state-designated campsites.
They are allowed to stay
for four days
before being forced
to move along.

The day after our happy time
with that Hawai'ian family,
the park ranger came to harass them.
Is he blind or just that venial?
He forced them to move on.
They loaded their things in an old car.
Moved to the next campground
to squat for four more days
in the land their gods gave them.

Warriors With Briefcases

My Cree ancestors pounded joyfully
across the plains.
Heading home
leading new horses.
Captured in a successful raid
upon their enemies.

My Metis ancestors fought valiantly
at Batoche.
To protect their home
against Canadian aggression.
A losing battle
against overwhelming odds.

My Gitxsan relatives made excursions
into the territory of others.
Approaching stealthily
in silently paddled canoes
to seize women, slaves,
precious possessions.

Today my warrior brothers
and sisters,
fight in boardrooms,
courtrooms,
armed with lawyers, briefs,
reports, injunctions.

Today we fight in
the court of public opinion
lead by PR men and women
armed with press releases.

We pit our small numbers,
our poor weapons,
against the unlimited resources,
coercive forces,
of industry, finance and state.

The battle tactics we choose
takes the form we call
active resistance.
They called it civil disobedience
at Oka, Gustafson Lake and Ipperwash.

I've stood upon the barricades.
Sat at road blockades.
Cooked and camped.
Done whatever's needed
to defend a way of life.

As I look into my child's deep, dark
trusting eyes,

I see the future.

Never doubting for a moment
what is right.

FISH WARS

Art sits deep in thought on the dark brown boulders
that disappear into the water's edge.

Deep muddy water roils by.
Cold fast waters.

Dangerous to human people.
An abundant home to the fish people
who traverse their underwater trails
from the ocean to their shallow creek birthplaces
by this river called Ksan.

The sleeping child upon my back.
The baby nestled in my belly, and me
step quietly back into the forest
so as not to disturb Art's contemplation of the floats of
the fish net lying on the water's surface.

Back in fish camp others wait.
Old people talk and laugh at ageless humour.
Women cook, preserve fish in the smokehouse.
Children squeal and roll on the dry grass.
Dogs lie sleeping in the dust.
Ears twitching flies away.

The CB radio crackles:
"They're coming."

My heart leaps.

Most of us go to the river.
Some to the road.

The police are coming in cars.
Fisheries officers
with police backup
coming up the river in jet boats.
A pincher movement.
A finely-tuned well-planned surprise attack.
We have followed its progress all day.

Don't they know that the moccasin telegraph
has gone electronic?

I am down by the river with my two babies.
Two old women, my *hlums*, Mary and Alice.
There are other women, children and old folks.
Only two or three men.

A dangerous group to confront police
and fisheries officers with jet boats
38s, shotguns, flak jackets.
The force of Canadian law behind them.

A self-important officer
sweltering in his flak jacket on
this hot summer day,
(Is the flak jacket to repel mosquitoes?
The most dangerous thing I see here today)
props his foot on the gunwale of his boat.

In a commanding voice,
he quotes a few statues we are offending.
Pronounces the immanent arrest of the net's owner.
Fishing deemed illegal by laws written last week
by people who do not own the river or the fish.

The officer grasps the expectedly heavy net,
heaves, falls backward into the boat
with a netless, fishless corkline.

All this finely-tuned well-planned
operation got today was
Toga gwats, a handful of shit,

Laughter echoing across the river.

INDIAN ART

"Indian Art"
a paradox.

We never did have a concept of art.
Yet we were ardently artistic.

We had useful things made beautiful.
With paint, quill, carving,
stone, bone, feathers.

Strangers came.
Gathered up our treasures.
Told us they were
of no value.
Bought them for a pittance.
Stole them outright
for their museums
and art collections.

As we searched for ways
to make a living
in our newly imposed reality.
We provided what the collectors
desired.
We could not understand.
What need has one for a chief's robe
who is not a chief?
Why would you want a quiver
if you do not hunt?
What use is this mask
if you do not dance?

Big business today.
Indian art.
At least for museums,
galleries, publishers.
Not for most of the creators
of these fine things.

For most Indian artists,
it's catch some fish
to jar.
Shoot a moose to freeze.
Work for wages for a few
weeks here and there.
Do a bit of artwork
to make a living.

For most of us
there's not much money
in it.

It's a way
to let our hearts sing
in a sometimes dreary world.

Creativity is one element
of the balance

for which all our souls hunger.

Alaska State Ferry

Ketchikan to Sitka.
Dolphins play in the sun-sparkled wake.

Gulls wheel and scream.
Shit joyously.

Pensioned south, forty-eight tourists
experience their wilderness adventures
from land-whale motorhomes.
Watching satellite TV
while dinner's in the microwave
among the cedars of this ancient shore.

A Forest Service employee boasts
"Alaska's bigger than Texas."

Blue and pink-haired ladies doze.
Tired from a day of extreme shopping in Ketchikan
where the jewelry is more extravagant
than Tiffany's.

Art lovingly created by native hands.

A few dollars paid.
Brings a shop profit.
Could have fed the artist's family
for a month.

Alaska where native communities
have been turned into corporations
by a beneficent liberal government.

The people once owners of the land
now are shareholders
I wonder if their naked ancestors
pulling strongly on their paddles
across this water
knew their future was

a for-profit enterprise?

ODE TO ENVIRONMENTALISTS

They read the words of Chief Seattle.
We too will live in harmony with the earth.
Like our native brothers and sisters
become environmental warriors.
Saving the earth from destruction.

The colonial society
are certain they get to determine
what the earth's agenda should be.

First on the list is vegetarianism.
We will save all our animal brothers and sisters.
They have feelings too.
A stroke of their philosophical pen,
they decide that every indigenous people
living north of the agricultural zone
never had a right to live.

The Inuit and Dene gone.

Next on the list are the cute little
white seal pups.
Their greatest success.
The market for seal destroyed
along with the Inuit hunters
who depended upon seals for their livelihood.

A rash of suicides among Inuit hunters.
Fathers, husbands, and providers
followed the end of the seal hide trade.
A little collateral damage can be expected
in every war.

Furs and trapping.
Also a very effective campaign.
Huge PR effort.
Throw blood on fur coats.
Distressed animals caught in traps
shown on TV.

The distress of native trappers,
hunting and trapping life on land,
deprived of their ancient way of life.

The foundation of their cultural existence,
unseen by the viewing audience.

The crowning glory of the environmental movement.
The anti-whaling lobby.
Whales are intelligent animals.
Whales are sentient beings.
Whales are so much like humans.

We should not kill them under any circumstance.

Whales are sentient beings
as are caribou, mice, mosquitoes and plants.
To our way of thinking,
all creatures are essential to the Creator's scheme.
Not just humans and whales.
We enter into relationships with animals.
Life displaces life
in a universal cycle.
We must all kill to live.
Even environmentalists.

If we do it with respect
we can continue to live.

The grand irony of the environmental
movement being
that members of the society who
have destroyed the earth
decide that we who destroyed nothing,
lived for millennia reciprocally with all,
cannot kill a whale, a seal or a fox.

One more aspect of colonialism.
One more form of genocide.

III: Rainbow Dancers

Little Elk Woman

Rainbow Dancer Child

sparkles,
shimmers in the sun.

Sun flashing on silver cones
as she dances.

Past, future,
hopes, dreams,
of parents, grandparents,
community and friends
People of all beliefs
and colours.

Little Elk Woman

a rainbow

in the sun.

Four Winds Woman

The face of a child.
Strength, depth, wisdom.

Movie stars and rock bands
are her superficial passion.

When others around her
go by the wayside.
Pitiable victims of seducing media,
drugs, men.

Four Winds Woman
will persist in her fortitude.
The wisdom of her ancestors
piloting her across the precipice.

The road is a difficult one
for our people.
I do not fear it entirely.

Four Winds Woman leading.

And a few others.

Will guide us to the future.

HOT SPRINGS RESPITE

A place full of life today.
Watchmen to guide,
keep order.
The elders to gather,
reminisce.
Families to visit and learn.
Visitors for curiosity and adventure.
Archaeologists to soak away weariness.

Dry, bright, sunny spot
Not like the rainy place we left.
the springs' sulfur dispels
the biting flies.
Not like the infested place we left.

The cedar bath house invites
the cold and tired.
My sweetheart and I soak naked
until our energy returns.
We leave the bath house
for the outdoor pools.
A temperature for every taste.
We choose the timid pool.

After the cold dark camp,
sitting in this hot pool
with a cool breeze upon our faces,
feels like paradise.

The rocky pool fed by the sulfur spring
flows over its edge in waterfalls
to the sandy beach below.

Sunlight sparkles
on blue green ocean waters.
Gulls wheel and slide overhead.

We soak until we wrinkle.
Join the others in the driftwood
shelter on the beach.
Eat halibut and West Coast scallops.

The elders bring the past alive.

We stay as long as we can
in this wonderful place.
Reluctantly board our boats.
Thread our way among the islands
to our wet work and dreary camps.

We are buoyed by the thought that
we will return to the Hot Springs soon.

THE MEANING OF EAGLES

One day in Haida Gwaii,
I saw eagles rising
from behind a hill.

Not flying
just drifting on the rising air
in great slow circles
around the hill.

More and more eagles appeared.

I was stunned by their numbers.
I tried to count them.

After fifty, it became impossible
to keep track.

Meaningless,
undesirable
to calculate this wonder.

There was deep meaning here.

Not in the eagles' number
but in their presence.

I asked a Haida elder
if she knew the meaning.

She said,
"The great birds are
honouring an Eagle Clan chief
who passed on to the spirit world
on this day."

HUMMINGBIRD POWER

The place was called Ka'kawis,
West Coast people's country,
Nuchanulth people's country,
West coast beauty.

We were on a healing journey
looking for strength, courage, love
within us.

The healing sweat
was part of the journey.

Departed that burning womb,
reluctant, rejoicing
to seek the cooling pool
at the foot of a little waterfall.

Stepped into those energizing waters
feeling life, strength,
power, spirit coursing through me.
Every drop of water sparkled
with an intensity I had never seen.
The ferns draped about the falls were burning green.
The smell of the earth was of the cycle itself.
Benevolent decay, joyous growth.
Fruitful provision.

I sucked in life from the earth, air, water,
cedars and ferns.
Another came to contribute to the gifts
that were inundating me,

Hummingbird came.

Two hummingbirds, male and female
sat impossibly on the edge of the falls.
They sat splashing and bathing as I did
filling my already-full heart with a singing joy.

The hummingbirds.
The world.
Life impossibly beautiful.

When the need arises
I remember that perfect moment.

BEADS

Glimmering, shimmering dancing
bits of rainbow.
Sewn, strung, tied on objects
of great beauty.

Capes, bags, moccasins, leggings.

Earrings, necklaces, staffs, bracelets.

Designed by loving hearts.
Created by loving hands
for one's loved ones.

Demanding whiteman's voice:
I want to know what the Indians did
before the whiteman brought glass beads.

We made beads of shell, horn,
bone and stone.

Coloured the quills the porcupine gave us.
with flowers, leaves and earth.

Painted beauty upon the skins.
Elk, Deer, Moose and Caribou gave us.

Then the whiteman came bearing
sparkling bits of rainbow.

A gift for which we give thanks.

DANCING

Skin, cloth, shell, glass, bone.
Sewn together with spirit, thought and care
Braided hair, eagle feathers.
Beads flash, fringes sway.

I dance the life-giving rhythm
of the heartbeat drum.
Mind moving faster than fringes.
Pray to the Creator giving thanks.
What a bad dancer I am.

I enjoy it anyway.

I think of past regrets, future plans.
Cultural appropriation.
Tourists stare with no appreciation,

I am proud of my careful sewing.
Embarrassed for a missed step.

I think of poor children
who hunger to dance.

Whose mothers have neither
the money nor the inclination to help them.
My ancestors danced before me.
My children will dance when I am gone.

The music, the rhythm,
all these bright things
are a great and beautiful gift
given us by the Creator.

IV: To Wound a Child

We Would Never Curse Your Children

Twenty-one tons of truck and logs,
roar through a once quiet village.
Children by the side of the road
cover their eyes
from the wind-driven dust swirls.

Parents worry that children and drivers
do not take enough care.
Parents fear that a precious child
may lose his life under those great wheels.

One of our own who is one of theirs,
working, loading the trucks with his machine,
hears on the radio,
"Damn, nearly hit one of those village kids!"

"Oh, well, one less to worry about for land claims."

For all the havoc and destruction
your society has wrecked upon ours.

Diseases that destroyed us.
The killing of our animals and plants.
Alcohol destroying our bodies and souls.

In spite of the devastation you brought

we would never curse your children.

ALEX

The dice are thrown.

A child is born
An achingly beautiful child.
A face of an angel child.
A bright child.
A lively child.
A little too lively sometimes.

Alex, you are going to hurt yourself.
Alex, you are going to break that.

School time.

Alex, sit down.
Alex, be quiet.

Still a beautiful child.
Generous.
Kind.
Loves everyone.
Can't fit the mold
of societal expectations.

The child becomes a young man.
More rules.

Alex, sit down.
Alex, be quiet.
Alex, do your homework.
Alex, come home on time.
Alex, don't smoke.

Alex, Alex, Alex!

What will happen to a man with

no education.
No job.
No direction.

In the old days
everyone was valued.
The mold made to fit the person.

His quickness would have made him a hunter.
His creativity, an artist.
His spirituality, a medicine man.

His kindness,
Beloved.

In our cookie-cutter world,

his differences make him

a throw-away.

Moccasins to School

Half breed girl.
Big city school.

Cotton print dress.
And moccasins.

Proud of those pretty moccasins.

Teacher says,

Who's that shuffling in
in her bedroom slippers?

Thirty years later
Still remember.
the humiliation and pain.

What gave her the right?

MOCCASINS TO SCHOOL AGAIN

Thirty years ago I learned the hard way
not to wear moccasins to school.

Times have changed.
Multiculturism
is official government policy.

People don't read the policy manuals.

Today a friend told me.
Her little boy in kindergarten
was so excited about
the moccasins his granny made him.

Home-tanned moosehide,
beaded moccasins.
Full of love, pride, sweat.

That little boy wore them everywhere,

proudly,

"Mommy, can I wear my moccasins
to school
to show my class?"

Same mistake I made
thirty years ago.

He came home from school.
Hid his moccasins.

"Where are your moccasins?"

"Teacher said they stink.
Shouldn't bring things like that to school."

Like my teacher thirty years ago.

Thinks she has the right

to wound a child
and his entire culture.

SUMMER SONG BOOK

Oscar called me the other day.
Anger and tears in his voice.

"My precious little daughter
came home from school today
with a Summer Song Book.
She had lovingly coloured the cover,
showed it to me with pride."

Teacher said,
"These are fun songs you can sing
around the camp-fire this summer."

"I looked at the songs.
I found in this multicultural,
anti-racist, politically-correct
society
a song that went like this:

'We are the red men.
Feathers in the head men.
Down in the ground.
Dead men.'

"I love my daughter
so much.
Want to protect her from evil

She is not even safe at school."

He wrote in response
an achingly eloquent letter
pouring out the centuries
of pain and injustice
suffered by the original peoples
of our country.

"Send the letter to the local paper.
It would be a service to the community.
A heart of stone would be touched by it.
Awareness will grow.
Racism will recede."

A great service to the community.

The community doesn't want to be served.
Racism is an entrenched position.

The citizens of this town want to believe
that native people are less than human.

They wouldn't print the letter.
Oscar's words will not be heard.

The Whitest Pocahontas You Ever Seen

What's this here?

It's a tumpline weaving loom
originally used to weave
mountain goat wool
into carrying straps.

In recent years commercial
wool has been used in them.

How'd you know this stuff?

I learned from my parents and grandparents.
Sought knowledge from elders in our community.
Learned from books written by
others who researched the topic.

Well, I'll be damned!
Hey, Bob!

Ain't she the whitest Pocahontas
you ever seen?

Bush Indians Hit the City

GITXSAN:
Win dii gay'iis di'gipaykwii.
(I've never been on an airplane before.)

Ne't loo'ii.
(Neither have I.)

Win dii gay'iis yee'ii.
(This is the first time I have gone to Vancouver.)

Gun nii.
(Me too.)
Soccer tournament is played.
Bush Indians take second place.

Let's celebrate.
Go downtown.
Meet some women.

Bush Indians move along
frantic city streets
in a nervous little knot.

Not knowing where they are.
Where they are going.

Looking for a little fun.

Ladies of the evening
on every corner.

"Why would we pay for it?
We get it at home for free."

"Here's a bar.
Let's have a victory beer.
Maybe we'll meet some women."

"Bartender, four beers, please."

Bush Indians relax.
Look around.

Dahl seexhl hanak?
(Where's the women?)

Duula wiltxw wilp oot.
(This is a gay bar.)

BUSH INDIAN IN THE CITY AGAIN

Soccer-playing bush Indian
returns to the city.

Waits in line for a restaurant seat.

Don't have to do this
at the Totem Cafe in New Town.

Strange people not seen at home.
Never seen before.

Ni'luu hanak dipuust.
(Those ladies sure are tall)

"That's because they aren't ladies."

"I really am a Crocodile Dundee."

The Dinner Party

I was born in the city but soon forgot.
Never hung with the right crowd.
Lived so long in the village I couldn't
remember other ways
I might have known.

Went back to the big city to go
to university.
Professor invites me for dinner.
Lucky a friend at school,
born into a middle class family,
knows all the rules.

"What should I do?"

"Bring a bottle of wine."

"To drink out of a paper bag?"

"No, to give to the hostess."

I am shocked.
Where I come from
drinking does not occur
in polite company.

Those who drink,
get blasted,
fight,
fall down.

We go to the party.
No one tells us how to get there.
What colour the house is
or the car outside.
We have an address with numbers.
A street name on a map.

A lady answers the door.
I give her the wine.
It's the wrong woman.

We sit on fine fancy furniture
in a spotless living room.
A filthy dog comes in,
slobbering, sniffing,
whacking over glasses
with his tail.
Why isn't he under the porch

where he belongs?

Everybody but me is drinking.
Wine, beer, liqueur, scotch, whiskey.
I keep waiting for the fight
to break out.
The booze is flowing.
Nobody gets drunk.
How do they do that?

It's time to eat.
I'm astounded.
The children are sitting
in the chiefs' places.
The chiefs are sitting
where the low-ranked should sit.
I am seated appropriately.
Even if no one but me knows it.

The party's over.
Walking the few blocks back
to my little room.
I see a very long bus that
bends in the middle
like an accordion.

Will city wonders never cease?

Last Night's Leftovers

Dad just moved to the village
used to a different world.
Early riser, up by five.
Coffee at the kitchen table
watching a sleepy village.

Dad says one morning:
"Good to see so many ambitious young men
going hunting and fishing so early in the morning."

Dad, those are last night's leftovers.

Confessions of a Mammoth Killer

Supermarket line up.

Interminable wait.

Wishing I could just go out

and kill something.

Not knowing soon I'd be accused
of just that.

Cute young cashier says,

"Oh, what a nice necklace.
What is it?"

"It's Raven carved in mammoth ivory."

"Well, that's not so nice then!"

"What?"

"Killing animals for their ivory.
Making them suffer for vanity"

"Mammoths have been extinct for 10,000 years
I didn't kill this animal."

"Oh, well, that's different then."

I collect my groceries.

Why do they pay people
who work in supermarkets
more than university professors?

VI: BROTHERS AND SISTERS

AAJU'S KITCHEN

I've seen some wonderful places.
Aaju's kitchen was among the best.

Windows all around bring the outdoors in.
Keeping it out at the same time.
Out is where a southern northerner like me
wants to keep a cold Iqaluit day.

Aaju's kitchen sits atop
a steep and rocky hill.
Snow-covered most of the year.

Snow machines roar up the hill
pulling *kamutiks*
laden with caribou and seal
 to eat and wear.

A dog team staked below
yaps a greeting to anyone who nears.

The sun shone every day
glittering off the snow
piled around her house.
the buckled tidal ice,
smother distant sea ice.

Caribou, a tasty but exotic treat,
seen only every few years
in my southern northern home
can be seen right out
Aaju's kitchen window.
On Aaju's kitchen table every day.

With great beauty all around
Aaju creates more beauty
with the magic of her needle.
Sealskins, black, grey and spotted.
Fox, white and silver-black.
Caribou, brown and white.
Wool and cotton, brightly coloured.

Aaju creates wondrous things.
Mitts, hats, coats, pants,
safety from the cold.

Beauty for the soul.

Are among the wonders in Aaju's kitchen.

BEAT AND EAT

We went to a place
where people gather with their sorrows,
a healing place on a healing journey.
Pain poured out of us from time to time.
We left with a lighter load.

I remember best
the joy of our recoveries
the sun-glittered sea from our windows.
The ravens feasting on our scraps
on an old cedar stump.

We gathered on the shore one shining day,
a picnic.
Some brought food from the store
fetched by boat.
The people of this place
gathered food from the sea.

At low tide these univalves clung tightly to the rocks.
A skilled hand with a knife could pry them free.
Their flesh was dark in colour,
a shellfish us northerners had never seen.

Sinking down upon the ground
our green plastic-bag clad hosts,
showed us how these shellfish are prepared.
They pounded the black meat
to edible tenderness,
dark red juice flying everywhere.

What are these?
The reply was unpronounceable
Nuchanulth
to our northern ears.
We resorted to that fine medium
of intertribal communication.
English.
But no one knew an English name.
A northern sister happily christened that shellfish
Beat and Eat on that joyful day.

Twenty Years Since I Looked Into Blue Eyes

Middle aged women
sit in a cafe having lunch.

Giggle and gossip
like young girls.

Husbands who drink too much.
Children with no direction.

Little hope

Jobs with hours too long.
Pay too short.

Responsibilities enough for ten.

One remarried recently.

Not a village man.
A different kind of man.

"It's been twenty years
since I looked into blue eyes."

They giggle.
Think of past flirtations.

What might have been.

What will likely be.

They dream.

CROSS-CULTURAL LOVERS

His mother very loudly doesn't say:
She's not white enough
she's not good enough.

Some white people put love in categories
race, class, age, socio-economic status
because everything can be measured and weighed
bought, paid for.
Even love.

Indians see people as they are
deserving of love
of value
love as an affair of two hearts.

What an affair it has been.
I've been young
but I didn't know incandescent passion
until I was 40.

We've settled into married life now
the differences are still there.

So is the passion
flaring now and then
in married lovers.

BROTHER MOOSE

Brother Moose,
I may smile at your awkwardness.
I mean no disrespect
you are our brother.

Like a brother
you protect us.
You nourish our bodies.
Give us your coat.
Insulate us from northland cold.

We honour you
using well every one of the gifts you give us.
We honour you.
By making objects of great beauty
with your sinew, hide and hair.

You give gifts to us
to sustain our body and soul.
We honour you.

PRAYER TO THE SWIMMERS

Beautiful Swimmers.

Silver flashing under sea dwellers.

The Human People welcome you.
You honour us with your presence.

We thank you, Chiefs,
for visiting our village.
Presenting us with
the gift of your own flesh.
Shedding your coats of flesh
for our sustenance.

We will honour you.
Greet you as great chiefs.
Call our people to receive you.
We will partake of your largess,
then restore every bone to the river.

So you can return to your homes
under the sea
to rest until next year.

You will don your coats of flesh again
to travel your trails beneath the river.

Bringing us your bounty once more.

VII: Is It Too Late to Give the Beads Back?

Is It Too Late to Give the Beads Back?

I love the beads the whiteman brought.

Peace comes to me in creating beauty with them.

What a price we paid for them.

Is it too late to give them back?

We Write in Other Ways

They say we were illiterate
until they brought us civilization.

The written word.
Even in this decade,
one of their officials said
we had "none of the badges of civilization."

The written word being one of them
wheeled vehicles being the other.

The scratchings of semi-literate
explorers and traders
outweigh the words of our great chiefs.

We write in other ways.

We write our histories
in the memories of our elders.

We write our knowledge of the land
in the minds of our hunters.

We write our values
in the hearts of our women.

We write in other ways.

Things they see as art.
Our chiefs robes and crest poles,
our lodge covers and quilled clothing
record messages plain to us.

Maybe we couldn't read their written words
when first they came.

But neither could they read ours.

We read their writings now.

Can they read ours?

WARD

Ward, my friend,
I knew your words before we met.
They inspired me, encouraged me.
Helped me to carry on in
the face of so much opposition.

Last year when you came to our school
we were excited to meet you.
To hear your words we knew so well.

You didn't disappoint us.
You are larger than ordinary people
in words, deeds and person.
As I gathered my family
to pick you up at our little airport.

"Oh no, I don't know what he looks like!"

A six-foot-five Indian in a elk hide jacket
stepped through the door.

It had to be you.

You didn't disappoint us.

You inspired us to renewed effort.
Harsh words for colonial oppression.
Kind words for all people.

You are what a man should be.

The Forestry Student in the Indians Hat

Lecture theatre.
Students and professors.
First class hypocrite former
environmental warrior
turned forest industry spokesman.

Debating.

Enlightened forester educated
by the academy, industry,
elders and the earth.

Called radical.

"There are only two rules to forestry:
Keep all the pieces.
If it doesn't feel right,
don't do it."

A man wise beyond his culture.

Forest industry town, forestry student,
forestry professors
debate in the guise of academic objectivity.
Deteriorates into racist arguments.

No special rights for Indians!
We're all Canadians
equal under the law!

Indians don't know anything about
conservation like
us industrial forest managers!

A student in a Cleveland Indians
baseball hat

"When do I get to be called native?
My family has been here three generations."

Two hundred people sat in that room.

Only a few understood the question.

THIRD WORLD CANADA

Canada is the greatest country.
A high standard of living.
No racism or poverty.
a land of freedom.
Opportunity for all.

No reason not to believe it.
It was true for him.

The years passed by.

His fate twisted this way and that.

He came to love a woman
of the First Nations.

She had a different story
from the one they told him.

He visited her reservation relatives.
Witnessed Third World conditions there.

Met people who could not feed their children.
Met people unwelcome in some places
for the colour of their skin.

Saw neighbours shun his children.

Saw people who had no hope at all.

Canada, you lied to him.

And to us all.

INDIAN BEAT REPORTER

Flying in like carrion-eaters,
chartered planes with big city, big newspaper money.
Indian beat reporters checking out the juiciest Indian
story.

Alcoholic racist doctor thirty years in this small town
curing, sometimes killing his native patients.
Why did he stay if he hated us so much?
Knew he couldn't do his drunken surgery elsewhere.

He's finally been brought to task.
An inquiry is being held.
A child's fearful, tearful parents brought her to that
physician.
"Take her home.
You people feed your kids too much candy."

She died of appendicitis before he could finish his
bottle.

Today the evidence is being examined.
I can't attend the inquiry,
work at the bar at 10:00 a.m.
When I open the door the usual hang-over hard cores
stumble in looking for their first drink of the day
held in two shaking hands.
The reporters follow close behind.

Evidence, reports, testimony, expert witnesses
are much too dull.
The reporters sit at the bar
ask whatever drunk to talk to them
in hope of a free beer, about the doctor.

The drunks ramble about past glories.
Does it matter what they or anyone else says?
The reporters had written the story before they arrived
before they descended from the sky.
The headline was
"White Versus Indian,"
tried, true story for increased circulation.

The newspaper arrived.
The headline proclaimed
"Inquiry Reveals Indian-White Spilt,"
the inquiry they never set foot in
with their predetermined assumptions.

Those who attended the inquiry heard the conclusion:
The doctor was found to blame in the child's death.
He is an alcoholic who should not work without other
doctors,
should get treatment for the alcoholism.
Won't lose his license.

The little girl is still dead.

BORN-AGAIN HEATHEN

When I was younger,
more patient and polite
I'd open my door in my housecoat
be friendly and courteous.
I've gained maturity
in more ways than one.
It comes in handy being a born-again heathen.
It makes Saturday morning
Jehovah's Witnesses
scuttle quickly away.

Closer to God

Dirty and drunken.
Despised and maligned.
The people of the street.
Native people in my town.

I sit in my warm comfortable home.
Drive by in my air-conditioned car.
See them sitting in doorways.
On bus benches.
Under trees.

How do they stay warm
when it's forty below?
What do they eat?
I give them a little money.

"Father, this is for You."

Will the five dollars buy
nourishing food
or poisoning booze?

Are they closer to God
sleeping out beneath the stars?

Are they closer to God
as they sit firmly on his creation?

What can I learn from them
as I live my plastic life
in concrete buildings

far above the earth.

DISEASES RARE AND COMMON

A hard working couple.

She and husband
walked the Red Road.

Made their people proud.

Suddenly, he died.

A rare disease consumed his flesh.

She forgot the Red Road.

Drowning her sorrows
in a bottle.

Couldn't take the loss
of that good man.

She died.

Of the most common disease
of our people.

But For the Grace of God

My work took me to a prison one time.

I met these men there.
Native guys.
All doing hard time.
Some lifers.

It was the saddest thing.
Most of them didn't remember the crime
for which they were doing the time

Alcoholic blackout.

Another sad thing.
One said he had to go to jail
to learn the things
he needed to know
to keep him out.

A frightening thing,
remembering the booze and drugs,
partying,
driving drunk.
All the bad shit I'd done.

Realizing that

There but for the grace of God went I.

Euphemisms of Silent Slaughter

Are you going out tonight?

Do you want a cold one?

Let's have a couple.

I had a few.

No matter how you say it.
No matter how you try to hide it.

It means death.
It's poison just the same.

Heard that an old Indian said

"Alcohol is a poison stronger
than the love of children."

I know it's true.

Many children are sacrificed
for the vile stuff.

Drink Like a Whiteman

I've been on a few healing journeys,
this was the first one.
We went to the home of the Kwagulth,
they taught us many things
we needed to follow the recovery path.

When we started to get a little stronger
our guide took us on a trip across the water
to another town,
a white town.
Where they too had their problems.

We sat in that meeting
heard the stories
of white alcoholics.
They often sounded like our stories,
stories of loss and grief,
the pain alcohol had caused them.

One among us said,
when I was young my parents said
drink like a whiteman.
Now I know
it's not Indian or white,
a drunk's a drunk.

APACHE ALLEY

A grimy town's dingiest street
Apache Alley.
Indians walk that street.
The down-and-out,
down-on-their-luck,
down-in-the-streets Indians.
Not teachers, lawyers or spirit men.
Stale beer-soaked bars,
greasy spoons,
strip joints.
Broken dream second-hand stores
and Indians.
Indians who don't remember the past,
won't remember the future,
remember they need a drink.

Do our proud Apache brothers
so many miles south
know that someone in this northern town
named our grimiest street
after Geronimo's grandchildren?

ANOTHER DEAD BABY

He's a man with a child of his own but
he's somebody's baby.
To his question:
Are you my baby?
His daughter replies:
You are my baby too Daddy.
Baby to his wife and lover.
His mother's baby still.

Good time Saturday night in an Indian country.
Boozing and cruzin'.

His life smashed out on the highway.

Bad booze.
Bad friends.
Bad driving.

Another dead baby.

The Ancient One

For ten thousand years you rested.
Not returning as your loved ones did.

Spring rains came.
River bank eroded.

You came out to see the world again.

Could you possibly have imagined
a world so changed?

That instead of leaving you
to return to the earth
of your own accord.

You were considered to be a great find.
A prize to be studied, dated.

Fought over.

Even the laws of the greedy ones declare
a box in a laboratory
should not be your destiny.

Your living descendants
should have a say in your fate.

The greedy ones have complicated rules.
Even their own can refuse to play.

You languish in that unhappy place,
your soul in torment.
The courts decide where your future lies.

Your relatives plead on moral grounds,

"Let us take him to his rest."

Have patience with us, Ancient One.

We will do right for you.

Black Glass

Born of trial by fire.

Beautiful, useful, desired obsidian.

An ancient Tahltan hunter ascends Edziza
picturing tools and weapons he will create.

Imagining the trades he will undertake.

The man sits among debris
left by previous obsidian seekers.
Striking glass with stone.

Adding to an accumulation that will become

A mountain ten thousand years hence.

The hunter brings his precious glass
down the mountain
to the village.
Finishes his tool
in the sun outside his house
to kill a caribou
to feed his children and his old ones.

Some of the cherished glass
he trades
to neighbours from the western sea.
They trade the inky stuff northward
to the people of the Icy Bay.

Three hundred generations pass.

Three hundred generations of hunters
strike stone on glass.
Three hundred generations build
a mountain of glittering volcanic debris.

I stand on that mountain.

Remember that ancient Tahltan hunter.

Archaeology Camp

Drive, ferry, boat, walk.

A long trip through space and time.

Look into the distant past.

We arrive.
The sun is shining.
The sky is blue.
The water sparkles.

The bugs are bad.

Set up camp.
Crawl into our tent
exhausted.

Awake to morning rain.
Gray and glowering sky.
Water, choppy slate.

The bugs are really bad.

Persistent mosquitoes.
Vicious black flies.
No-see-ems penetrating the impenetrable.
Earwigs crawl into everything.

Elders tell stories from the past.
The flood ten thousand years ago.
The world was not as it is now
when Raven walked this shore.

We seek the record
laid in the ground
in stones rendered
by our ancestors' hands.

We seek places where
they camped
as we do today on this beach.

Will archaeologists ten thousand
years from now
know what we did here?
We presume to know what our ancestors did
in the camps we find.

Bugs try to chew my bones.

Carefully,
we dig the earth,
screen the dirt.

We find many small relics
of those ancient times.

We find vivid reminders of the past.
Biface and microblade
carefully made by a craftsman
of that distant time.

Did he think of the past
as he held this stone
in his hand?
Think anyone would care
about his broken, discarded tool?

Know it would tell his story
in ten thousand years?

If I could have one wish
I would wish to travel back
to meet the craftsman.
Find out if his life was as I imagine it.

Were the bugs as bad as now?

PEOPLE OF THE WOLF AND RAVEN

The people of the Wolf and Raven
were the first to walk this land.
They came here as the ice was melting.
Where there had been no other band.

The land was new as spring
no trees were growing yet.
The land was not as now.
But its ownership was set.

Mammoths, sloths, giant beavers.
Wolves and Ravens hunted them.
Passed from the land as winds grew warm.
Never to be seen again.

Moose, caribou, bear became
food and clothing for those old ones
who then moved into river canyons
to fish the salmon runs.

Ten thousand years or more have passed
since the Wolves and Ravens came
The world has changed so greatly.

Their land is still the same.

T'XEMLAX'AMID

The White People call it mythical.
I've seen it.

The White People call it legendary.
I've been there.

Thousands of years ago.
The People settled across
the river from Stekyoodenhlxw.
Three long rows of houses
in the widening of the valley.

The People prospered.
The Fish People, Goat People, others,
provided for the Human People.

So long as they showed respect.

Three times the Human People erred
forgetting the law of respect.

The Mountain Goat People took their revenge.

Abuse of the Trout People brought the *Medik*.

The People recovered.
T'xemlax'amid went on.

Then came the third transgression
against the Spring Salmon People.

It spelled the end of T'xemlax'amid.

The People were cast out.

The diaspora took them to distant places.
Today their descendants in many nations
tell how their ancestors' time at T'xemlax'amid

ended with a snowfall in summer.

DAUGHTER OF THE METIS NATION

Who are the Metis?
There are as many answers
as there are Metis.
Each story is complex.
The sum of the stories create our nation.

A history teacher once told me:
Your family history is
the history of the Metis.
The eleventh generation
descendent of Pierre and Anne Piche
came to Quebec from France.
Nearly 350 years ago.

The granddaughter
of Joseph Oulette of Quebec.
Who married an Indian woman
they named Angelique,
began the building of the Metis Nation.

The granddaughter of Michel Pattenaude
born "somewhere east of Lake Superior in 1784,"
his Innu wife Marguerite Serpente
went west to Red River.

The granddaughter of the Red River buffalo hunter
Joseph Piche,
his Lakota wife they called
Suzanne White Horse.

The granddaughter of many generations
who struggled to create
the Metis nation at Red River.
Piches, Ouellettes, Bremners
Taylors, Tucottes and Pattenaudes.

The granddaughter of the mediators between
our Indian and white relatives
in the Northwest fur trade.
The granddaughter of the people of St. Boniface
St. Eustache, St. Francais Xavier.
The granddaughter
of Governor Simpson's country wife Margaret
forsaken for a real wife, a white wife.

The granddaughter of Louis Pattenaude
who fought with Big Bear
when the Cree and Metis
tried to stop the invasion of their land.

The granddaughter of people
who received the government's
empty promise of scrip.

The granddaughter of the Metis
who stayed in Red River
until the starving times of the '30s.

The granddaughter of the people
who continued their westward migration
seeking survival, hope and future.

I am the daughter of the Metis nation.

Forty Year Cycle

I met a man in Vancouver
from a village in the north.

A kind and funny man.

We made plans
to move to his village.
To marry.

We were to leave the city
when that man was struck down
by a crazy woman with a knife.

Soon he was recovering.
He said "Go on ahead.
I'll be there."

Before I left
for that northern village
I visited my grandmother.
Told her where I was going.

"Kispiox!" she said,
"Comer took me there
forty years ago.
His mother was a Starr.

"It was summer.
Hot dust in the summer air.
As we crossed the bridge
There was a little boy
watching the lazy
summer-shrunken river.
The dogs and him.
The only signs of life.

"The houses were boarded up.
Comer said they had gone
to the coast
to pack their fish into
the whiteman's cans.

"Now you are marrying
a man from there too.
Isn't that funny."

That man I was to marry
never did come home.
He wrote many fine letters
of loving words.
Finally admitted,
"I can't come back.
I'm a city Indian now."

I couldn't go home either.
I was a village Indian then.

I married another man
from that small village.

Raised three children there,
forty years after my grandmother
crossed that bridge
to her husband's ancestral home.

Later my *hlums*, Mary, told me
"Those who come to live here
were meant to.

Their souls were from here.

Wandered and came home."

GRANNY JESSIE

Part I

I called my grandmother Jessie.
Don't know why.

Fourteen years old,
she stepped off the steamship
from Scotland.
New, beautiful, full of hope.
With mother Bec, father Jock,
brother Bill.

They were lured to Red River
with the promise of farm land aplenty.
Government failing to tell them
it was someone else's home.

Four years later Jessie married
Fred Pattenaude, old Red River
Metis family.
Tall, handsome, raven eyes and hair
Jessie hadn't been here long enough
to know.
White women don't marry half-breed men.

She found out soon enough
as she waited with fading hope
for the white neighbour women
to put up a wedding shower.

Fred's people were kind to Jessie.
Loved her all her life.
Even if Fred was not, did not.
They fed her from the land
when the farming failed.

1931
Jessie bore a dark-eyed babe,
my mother, Claire Irene.

1936
Desperation drove them west
to the promise of West Coast dock work
where Indians were welcome.

Jessie bore Fred two more daughters,
Patti and Diane.
Marriage ended.

Life went on.

Part II

1953
I am born to Claire and Alex.
Many young hours in Jessie's
huge beautiful house.
So friendly and inviting.
Granny Bec and Jocky lived upstairs.
Granny Pattenaude around the corner.

Jessie had a second husband
no better than the first.
She sewed to make a living.
Family swirled in and out
of that big house.

1968
Granny Bec passed.
Jessie cared for Jocky to
the end of his 96 years.

Granny Pattenaude joined
her ancestors at 96.
Jessie got a little place of her own.
Family still flowed in and out.
I miss that big house and all it meant.

Jessie lived to see two great grandchildren
Then the piper piped her away.

She is far from forgotten.
Lives on in my prayers and dreams.
Lives on in the unfathomable eyes
of my third child.
My little Jessie.

Granny Jessie.
A strong and steadfast woman.
I love her still.

Petty Crap and Winter Birds

Working, moving, fighting with my husband.
Stress created by every little thing.
My life on the verge of implosion
under the weight of petty crap.

No time for important things
like playing with my children.
Creating things of beauty.

As I rush from one obligation to the next
I catch a glimpse of winter birds
in a leafless tree.

Fat little brown birds
fluff their feathers against winter's cold.
I take the time to watch them.
Am better for it.
A few minutes from my hectic schedule
renews me.

The birds confirm
that nature waits patiently
despite my fretful existence.

As my schedule slips from my mind
I feel the breath of Mother Earth
who lies quietly beneath the concrete.

I thank her for her gift
of fat brown winter birds
in a leafless tree.

A little harmony has been restored,
I move on with my hectic life.

FAILED WARRIOR

Where is that warrior woman?

Striding through life.
Righting wrongs.
Overcoming oppression.
Soaking up wisdom
for the good of the people.

Who is this?

Arguing with husband over money.
Striving to buy
the American Dream for daughter.
Bailing out son charged with theft?

Where is that warrior woman?

Sobering every drunk.
Watched her Dad die of drink.
The father of her children
sits in a bar.
He's supposed to be at the circus.

She wants to end fifteen years
of sobriety
slink off to a sleazy bar.
If everyone would promise
not to talk to her.

Where is that warrior woman?

Living in a bush camp.
Cutting up a moose.
Smoking a thousand fish
for a long cold winter.
Tanning hides for the family's clothing.

Complaining the thermostat's too low.
The price of beef too high.

Where is that warrior woman?

Spending her days with village elders.
Absorbing their wisdom.
Some day becoming them.

In her office.
Reading a book.
Pretending she knows something.

Where is that warrior woman?

Will she rise to fight again?

Or has she been defeated by

dirty dishes, dirty laundry,
dirty politics, dirty lies?

ACADEMIC INDIAN'S TRAVEL REQUIREMENTS

The whiteman ain't all bad.
Some of my best friends are.

They bought us
the essential tools for
academic Indian life.

The laptop.
The pickup.
The bank card.

I don't leave home without 'em.

XI: THE LAND SPEAKS

XSAN'S STORIES

Northland river.
River of mist.
Reveal to me your stories.

Great river.
You are much more than water.
The people's life has revolved
around you.
Since the beginning of time.

They have called themselves
after you.

Gitxsan, People of Xsan.

Great river.
You, like the people
and other animals
have had many incarnations.

Great river.
Before this lifetime
you lay locked
in a vast sheet of ice.

As the summers warmed
the ice released you.
At the beginning of this life
you were a wild thing.
Choked with ice and gravel.
Glacier-ground.

Great river.
You struggled to find
your old pathway.
The people began to appear
on your banks.
Seeking new lands to live on.
Finding a rapport with you.

Great river.
The ice and gravel washed to sea.
You settled comfortably
into your rocky bed.
The people paddled your waters.
Walked your shores.
Built their villages beside your bounty.

Great River.
Generous.

Providing the people
with the twin staffs of life

The salmon which traverse
your underwater trails each year.
The versatile cedar from your shores.

Great river.
You have flowed through the millennia.
You have witnessed a thousand stories.
Some you have revealed to me today.

I sit on your sun-dappled bank
Contemplating
your roiling gray flow to eternity.

WOMAN CHOPPING WOOD

I asked Nancy about the old days.

Research.

She wasn't that old.
Fifty something.
She knew a lot.

She had an old-time marriage.
Young girl honoured by
union with a great chief.

She was twenty.
He was sixty.
He weakened with age.

She grew stronger.

In the old days the family
lived together.
Would have supported Nancy,
her children, her elderly husband.

Her husband passed away.
So did the old days.

Nancy grew even stronger.

Had to look after herself.
All those kids.

The day I went to see her
she was chopping wood
with great skill and ease.

When I try to split a log
it usually flies off the chopping block.

I was grateful
I had a husband to do that work.

Still think about Nancy.
Her toughness and independence.
How she went out onto the land
to make a living for herself
and her children.

How she could kill and pack a moose.
Setting traps alone for money
to buy flour and tea.
How the smoke was always rising
from her smokehouse.

When the tribal council
was mapping the people's land
they took Nancy up in an airplane
to name her hunting grounds.

The pilot was amazed.
She charted that uncharted territory.
Before crossing over every hill,
she named what was on the other side.

She named every hill and creek.
Every river, rock and mountain.

Her land was etched in her mind
from walking every trail and stream.

From the stories her grandparents told.

The memory of centuries
of her ancestors on the land.

As I watched her chopping wood
I wondered if Nancy's daughters
with their busy modern lives

have that land mapped in their minds.

DEH CHO

Away in the big steel winged machine
Edmonton to Inuvik via
Yellowknife and Norman Wells.
The airplane drones northward
streaking through the sky
as our ancestors would never
have dreamt.

Below I see a tough land
in late November's winter grip.
not the voluptuous cedars
of my West Coast youth.
Small hard spruce,
a million frozen lakes and streams,
rocks and snow.

No sign of the habitants from
thirty thousand feet.

Stretching out before me
I see a mighty river.
A broad and frozen silver ribbon.
Undulating to the Arctic sea.

This River called MacKenzie
by the arrogant whitemen.
Named the river after one of their own
who briefly stumbled through here
cold and hungry.

This river is Deh Cho.

The heart of Dene land.
Since mammoth and giant beaver walked.
People werc animals.
Animals were people.
When Yamoria shaped this land.

And Raven played his tricks.

For ten thousand years
this river has been Deh Cho.

Tahltan

Iskut village in
spruce and birch country.
Winter come early country.
Tahltan country.
Nestled below a towering peak
I can almost see the caribou
from here.

My Tahltan friend takes me north to Dease.
Same subarctic country.

At Dease we head west on a gravel road.
The country begins to change
Dry plateau country.
Sage and juniper country.

The road follows the Stikine.
A deep cut, many canyoned river.
We stop to absorb the beauty,
stand on cliffs that drop
long and sharply to the rough waters.

We approach
the Tahltan–Stikine confluence.
A stunning sight.
Two great rivers flow parallel for a distance.
The road perched precariously between them.
Paved over the ancient trail.

On the narrow towering strip of rock
standing in one place I can see
a river on either side of me,
hundreds of feet below.

We travel the tight switchbacks
dropping quickly down to the canyon floor.
Two old smokehouses stand in the narrow valley.
Several small houses.
Many Tahltan come here in summer.

The past comes alive in Tahltan Canyon.
For ten thousand years and more
The Tahltan have come to this canyon
to catch and dry their year's supply of salmon.
As they did just yesterday.

KLAPANA

Patches of forest and tundra alternate
as we gingerly drive this rough road.

Fearing a punctured tire.

Locals in high-riding trucks with big tires.
Many seasons of experience on this track
roar by with a wave and a cloud of dust.

As we climb, the forest gives way to unbroken tundra.
Scrub willow, berry bushes, red and purple
wildflowers.
A few hours of picking our way around potholes
our destination appears across a wide valley.
A camp where generations of hunting families
have made a living.
Seeking out caribou and moose
goat and sheep, groundhog and ptarmigan.

Today three more generations do the same.
Kids with slingshots carefully carved
by Grandfather Robert
bring down tasty ptarmigan
while their fathers bring down caribou with 303s.

The camp so clean and comfortable.
A place where this kind of life
has been carried on for a long time.

That's the idea.

To carry on.

To live as Tahltan have lived for generations.
Will continue to live.

I didn't want to leave that place.

Alfred's Story

New job.
Important job.
Researcher.
No slinging beer
anymore.

The boss:

"Here's your office.
Do genealogies."

Good thing I got stuck
with that kinship course in college.
Digging through records.
Figuring out who to talk to.

Alfred visits

A chief, an elder, a researcher,
knowledgeable in every way.

Alfred told me a story that belies
the 'nasty, brutish and short' epitaph
applied to pre-European-contact
aboriginal life.

"My grandmother told me
that she was young
living in Hagwilget.
Her grandmother said,

'We'll go to Kitwancool
to visit our relatives.'

They walked the forty miles.

When they reached the village
they approached a big red cedar house.
Outside sat a very old man.
So old his back bent right over.
He walked leaning on two canes.

He was the young girl's
grandmother's
                grandfather.

They went inside the house
to meet his mother.

The ancient lady was so old.
Her body withered with time.

She barely made a bump
beneath her blanket.
She no longer had the strength
to hold her head up when she spoke.
She rested her chin on a rest
lovingly carved by those
who still wished to hear
her words of wisdom.

Her body was a memory of its former vigour.
Her mind was as clear as in her youth."

Alfred thought the lady
might be one hundred fifty.
His grandmother's
          grandmother's
                    grandfather's
                              mother.

Many times I hear of elders
dancing, hunting, fishing, curing,
raising children
in their second century.

With Alfred's story disappeared
the least tendency I ever had
to believe what they told me in school

about Indian life being nasty
brutish and short.

PERCY'S STORIES

Gee-zus Cur-ist! I never gonna forget
what I seen as long as I live.

Percy's lived his long life.
Gone on to the spirit world now.
Left his stories with me.
His words hang in my mind
in his blue room.

"Gee-zus Cur-ist!
Me and Joe was 'bout sixteen.
We was sneakin' aroun'.
Out by where the *halaits*
had their place at Anlax.

They had a ol' log cabin.
They was a bunch of them inside.
We was lookin' through the cracks.

They was dressed up.
Bear skins, bear claws,
'roun their necks,
on their heads.

Aprons, *aatai asxw* an' stuff.
They dance, sing, rattle, drum.
Got a fire in the middle
o' that dirt floor.

They got Mathilda there.
She been sick a year or so
She dressed up like them *halaits*.

One ol' *halait* spread out
the hot coals.
into a path 'bout eight feet long.
I start to get real scared
'Joe, what they gonna do?'

'She gonna walk on it.'

Mathilda in her bare feet.
She walk on them burning coals.
She drag her feet real slow
through them coals."

Percy shuffled his hands in the air.

"Them ol' *halaits* keep singin', drummin',
rattlin', dancin'.

Mathilda, she go slowly,
slowly through them red hot coals.

I get the hell out of there.

Later, me and Joe, we ask her,

'What's it feel like?'

She say, 'They tell me
it's *siiyum*-glacier.
It feel like ice.'

Gee-zus! That's one thing
I couldn't get over.

I never gonna forget that."

Printed and bound
in Boucherville, Quebec, Canada by
MARC VEILLEUX IMPRIMEUR INC.
in September, 1999